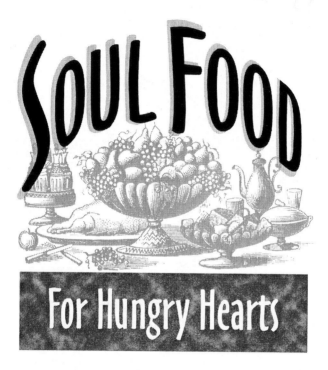

SOUL FOOD

For Hungry Hearts

By
Patricia A. Outlaw, Ph.D., D. Min.

GATEWAY PRESS, INC.
Baltimore, MD   2005

Please direct all correspondence and book orders to:
Patricia A. Outlaw, Ph.D., D. Min.
828 Castlemaine Dr.
Birmingham, AL 35226

Library of Congress Control Number 2004116121
ISBN 0-9764704-0-3

Published for the author by
Gateway Press, Inc.
1001 N. Calvert Street
Baltimore, MD 21202-3897

www.gatewaypress.com

Printed in the United States of America

Soul Food for Hungry Hearts is dedicated to

The memory of Arthur Outlaw
The living testimony of Isabelle Rich
My Sister Cojourners
&
All the beautiful people
who grew up with me in Sandtown.

Contents

Introduction

Soul Food for Hungry Hearts is a book of sermons. These sermons were written and preached by the author with hungry people in mind. Many people have been suffering from spiritual obesity or spiritual anorexia. The spiritually obese have more than enough to eat, but they continue to overindulge themselves by eating enormous amounts of foods that are not providing them with the right mix of spiritual nutrients. While the spiritually anorexic refuse to taste and see that the Lord is good. Spiritual anorexics choose not to come to the banquet table and partake of daily bread which is necessary for sustaining a healthy, abundant lifestyle.

These sermons challenge the reader to go deep within herself and to examine her own specific nutritional requirements. Some readers will discover that they need to eat foods which will speed up their metabolism. Other readers will learn to create space in their lives to be still and sit at the feet of the Master Chef. Many other readers will learn to appreciate the value of adding the disciplines of spiritual exercise to their menu.

Chapter one, "No Place for a Grasshopper Mentality," will encourage readers to do some, serious, self-analysis and examine their past patterns of behavior. Chapter two, "Get out the Kitchen," will challenge the reader to consider another alternative to spending excessive amounts of time in the kitchen with the pots and pans. Chapter three, "Do your Part," is intended to help the reader empathize with others and invites her to give something back to the community. Chapter four, "You've Got the Power," equips the reader to use her gifts to spread the Good News to others. Chapter five, "Your Will be done," teaches the reader to surrender her appetites to God. Chapter six, "Lead Us Not into Temptation," encourages the reader to go to whatever lengths necessary to finish the race. Chapter seven, "Call Me by My Name," affirms each person's own destiny and shows her or him the power of using God's name, so that times of refreshing will come.

Soulfood for Hungry Hearts was written for women and men. However, the women and men who attended the Women's Prayer Convocation, sponsored by the 5th Episcopal District of the African Methodist Episcopal Church in Albuquerque, New Mexico, May 12–16, 2004, under the leadership of Bishop John R. Bryant and Episcopal Supervisor, Dr. Cecelia Williams Bryant were the impetus for this book. Many of the participants at the Women's Prayer Convocation asked the author for written copies of her sermon, "Call Me by My Name." The writer offers this book as a gift of love to those sisters and brothers who danced with God at the Holy Communion Service on May 16. This is her way of responding to their requests and sharing with others who have not heard her preach.

1 | No Place for a Grasshopper Mentality

"We saw the Nephilim there (the descendants of Anak come from the Nephilim). We seemed like grasshoppers in our own eyes, and we looked the same to them."

(Numbers 13:33, NIV)

In his book, *The Mis-education of the Negro*, the sagacious Carter G. Woodson wrote,

When you control a man's thinking you do not have to worry about his actions. You do not have to tell him not to stand or go yonder. He will find his "proper place" and will stay in it. You do not need to send him to the back door. He will go without being told. In fact, if there is no back door, he will cut one for his special benefit. His education makes it necessary.[1]

Woodson understood that mind control is an intentional and systematic strategy to take control of another person's cognitions.

The goal of controlling another person's thinking is to make them believe what you want them to believe and do what you want them to do. Several factors may contribute to a person's susceptibility to brainwashing. Sensory deprivation of one kind or another makes the individual vulnerable. If a person is deprived of food, light, sleep, shelter, and companionship for extended periods of time, she may yield to the dictates of an oppressor.

Holocaust victims, prisoners of war, and African-American slaves have been the subjects of intentional mind control. Held captive against their wills, these persons were robbed of their dignity, identity, and self-esteem. They lived in deplorable conditions, were deprived of the basic necessities for sustaining life, and were treated as property. As a result of the malevolent treatment of their oppressors and the trauma associated with enslavement, the survivors of the holocaust, war, and American slavery, and by extension their descendants, developed a post-traumatic slavery syndrome.

Post-traumatic slavery syndrome is a spiritual and psychological disorder. It is spiritual because the survivor navigates through life from a deprivation mentality. Her image of herself is distorted. She is confused about who she is and whose she is. She cannot comprehend how a loving God would permit such a dastardly thing to happen to her. Her self image becomes confused with the image of the oppressor. She resists seeing herself as made in the image of God. Rather, she *introjects*, psychologically speaking, the self image of the oppressor and attempts to be like the one who keeps her in bondage.

Not only is post-traumatic slavery syndrome spiritual, it is also psychological. The trauma of incarceration, isolation, and deprivation keeps the individual in a psychological state of anxiety, self-doubt, confusion, and delusion. Feelings of insecurity, abandonment, rejection, and fear take the place of acceptance, trust, confidence, and affiliation. The attitude of the post-traumatic slavery, syndrome sufferer is one of passive acceptance, misperception, self-denigration, and paranoia. Thus, it may be difficult for persons with post-traumatic slavery disorder to live normal, hopeful lives, because their vision of reality is clouded by their prior negative experiences.

Similarly, the Israelites during the time of Moses seemed to show some signs of post-traumatic slavery syndrome. They allowed others to control their thoughts, and their image of themselves. Let us zoom our sermonic spotlight on to our text, Numbers 13: 33. "We saw the Nephilim there (the descendants of Anak come from the Nephilim). We seemed like grasshoppers in our own eyes, and we looked the same to them." In retrospect the Israelites suffered deep psychological and spiritual wounds at the hands of their Egyptian captors. According to Exodus the Israelites were oppressed and forced into captivity.[2] Their family life was disrupted by Pharaoh's order to assassinate all of their male infants with the sole intention of eliminating the next generation. The Israelites were deprived of the basic necessities of life, robbed of their dignity, depleted of their internal resources, made to feel like unwanted, dependent children. To make matters worse they were ordered to make bricks without straw.[3]

In their despair the Israelites cried to the Lord, and the Lord heard their cry. Yahweh showed the Israelites mercy and rescued them from Egyptian bondage. The Lord God sent ten plagues to Egypt to soften Pharaoh's hard heart. But Pharaoh's heart was blocked with self-will and arrogance. He refused to let the people go.[4] However, the sovereign God opened up the Red Sea with a mighty wind which held back the waters, and the Israelites walked through the sea on dry land. The Egyptians were swallowed up by the returning, rushing waters.[5] God intervened once again in the lives of the Israelites, brought them through forty years of wandering in the wilderness to the banks of freedom.

The book of Numbers greets us with the liberated Israelites

about to cross over into the promise land. These same people who had been delivered from the Egyptians by an almighty God were about to fall prey to their post-traumatic slavery disorder. They were about to doubt God and believe the negative thoughts of their persuasive peers.

The Lord told Moses to send some scouts ahead to explore the land of Canaan, "which I am giving you."[6] Note the use of the present tense. In other words the Lord said that the land is yours now. Go check it out and claim it. Moses sent out leaders from the twelve tribes of Israel to explore the land. Moses said, "Go up there and see what the land is like." See if the people are strong or weak. Investigate their resources, bring back some fruit, so we can get some idea of what to expect.

The Bible says, Numbers 13:21–29, that the men went up and explored the land. The land was fruitful. But the men came back with two different reports. Brothers, Caleb and Joshua came back with an optimistic report. Caleb told Moses, "We should go up and take possession of the land for, we can certainly do it."[7] The other group of men said, "No, we can't attack those people, they are stronger than we are."[8] These men fed into the Israelites fears. They manipulated them by telling them that the people they saw in Canaan were of a great size. They were so strong and tall that they, the Israelites, seemed like grasshoppers in their own eyes and in the eyes of the Nephilim.[9]

The Israelites quickly forgot about the sovereign God who delivered them from Egyptian slavery and brought them through the Red Sea. Instead they bought into a grasshopper mentality. Since the men with influence told them that they looked like grasshoppers compared to the enemy, they believed what they were told. They started acting like grasshoppers. How do grasshoppers act when they feel threatened? They jump from one place to another. They don't pay much attention to where they land; they just jump. The Israelites jumped back into their old method of coping.

They started whining and grumbling against Moses and Aaron. They threatened to stone their leaders to death. But then the glory of the Lord appeared to Moses. And the Lord said, "How long will these people treat me with contempt ... in spite of all the miraculous signs I have shown them? I will strike them down with a plague."[10] They are not going to come into the promise land with a grasshopper mentality.

God forgave the Israelite people at the request of Moses for their sin against him. However, even though they were forgiven, they paid a price. None of the adults over twenty-one were allowed to see the promise land. God told them that no one who has treated me with contempt will ever see it. However, Caleb has a different spirit and follows me wholeheartedly, I will bring him into the land, and his descendents will inherit it. There is no place in the promise land for a grasshopper mentality.

What might we learn from this story? First we need to know who we really are. We are not grasshoppers. We don't have to jump, because others tell us to jump. We are made in the image and likeness of God. We belong to the King. And as children of the King we ought to trust that he has already provided an inheritance for us. Second, God always keeps his promises. If he says that he is going to give you the land, then trust God to do what he says he is going to do. He may not come when you want him to come, but he is always on time. Turn off the negative voices which tell you that you are a grasshopper. Third, remember God is still sovereign. He is reigning supreme on the throne of glory. God wants to expand your territory by taking you to the promise land. There is no place in Canaan for a grasshopper mentality, so get over it.

I will close with a personal story. I was born out of wedlock. At the time of my birth my mother had the progressive foresight to write my father's name on my birth certificate and to insist that I also be given my father's last name, rather than her last name.

Even though I did not grow up in my father's house, we managed to have a good father-daughter relationship. I was his only child, and he told me that one day I would inherit his portion of the land in North Carolina which had been left to him by his mother.

Daddy died in 1975. When I attempted to claim my share of the land, I was told at that time, that I was not eligible under North Carolina law, because I was "illegitimate." I left that decision in God's hands and moved on with my life. In the year 2000, twenty-five years later, one of my cousins decided to build his retirement home on what he believed was his portion of the land. He was required by new North Carolina laws to have the land surveyed. All likely heirs had to be notified and the land divided accordingly. My cousin's lawyer contacted me in Baltimore. For the record my father lived most of his life and died in Baltimore.

Since my father lived and died in Baltimore, his estate was governed by Maryland law. Maryland law stated that if your father, publicly and notoriously recognized you as his child, then you were legally, and morally deemed to be his child and entitled to his inheritance. My cousin's lawyer asked me to send him a copy of my birth certificate and any photographs of me with my father and other family members. I sent the lawyers the requested documents. In the year 2000 I received my official deed for my share of the heir property.

There is no secret what God can do. God always keeps his promises. Jesus died on the cross for us. He took our low self-esteem, our sins, our traumas, and our illegitimate status to the cross with him. We have been healed by his blood. On Resurrection Sunday Jesus got up from the grave with all power in his hands. And because he got up, we can get up too. In the words of Martin Luther King, Jr., "I have been to the mountaintop, and I have looked over into glory. I have seen the promise land. I may not get there with you, but I will get to the promise land."

6

2 | Get Out the Kitchen

As they continued their travel, Jesus entered a village. A woman by the name of Martha welcomed him and made him feel quite at home. She had a sister, Mary, who sat before the Master hanging on every word he said. But Martha was pulled away by all she had to do in the kitchen. Later, she stepped in, interrupting them. "Master, don't you care that my sister has abandoned the kitchen to me? Tell her to lend me a hand." The Master said, "Martha, dear Martha, you're fussing far too much and getting yourself worked up over nothing. One thing only is essential, and Mary has chosen it—it's the main course, and won't be taken from her."
(Luke 10:38–42, The Message)

Our nation which was founded under the banner of "one nation under God," is under distress. September 11, 2001 and the invasion of Iraq in 2003 has left memories of destruction, distrust, and despair in the psyche of survivors. Deferred dreams turned into nightmares. Not only is the nation under stress, but our churches are under stress as well.

Clergy have left their pastoral charges in large numbers, because they can no longer handle the malaise of their parishioners. Too often, they have been seared by the scorching heat of burnout without realizing that they had been standing in a pot of lukewarm water which was gradually increasing in temperature.

Missionaries travel from other world countries to evangelize Americans, because many of us suffer from biblical illiteracy, and we no longer herald the motto "in God we trust" which is blazed on our dollar bills. George Barna's research underscores the lack of biblical literacy in the church. He also suggests that there is a lack of a passionate pursuit of a lifestyle which is consistent with the mission of Jesus Christ. Many Christians don't live like Christians, because they don't know what they believe. Therefore, they are unable to apply scripture to their lives. Since most non-Christians don't read the Bible, they judge Christianity by the lives of the Christians they see. It may very well be that the church has been spending too much time on appetizers and not enough time on the main course. With that thought in mind we will use as our theme for this chapter, "Get Out the Kitchen."

Our text introduces us to two sisters, Mary and Martha, who like many siblings, were in temporary conflict about what was the priority of the present moment. Ben Witherington, the author of *Women and the Genesis of Christianity* states, "Mary and Martha may have been the most important and prominent women in Jesus' life after his own mother."[11] Martha who is mentioned first in the text welcomed Jesus into their Bethany home. Without a doubt Mary must have been excited to see Jesus too, because the Bible says that she sat at the Lord's feet listening, hanging on every word. The fact that Mary "sat at the Lord's feet" was highly significant for a Jewish woman during that time in history. It was common for Jewish men to sit at the feet of their teachers, but not women. But in the text we find Mary, a female, sitting at the feet of Jesus. This was notably irregular, especially since women were not allowed to study the scriptures with a rabbi. Most rabbis would not have entertained Mary as Jesus did, even in the privacy of her own home. Yet, there she was sitting at the feet of Jesus hanging on every word. Jesus broke with tradition and culture when he permitted Mary to sit at his feet. In that historical moment he affirmed a woman's right to study his word and be his disciple. He supported her interest in spiritual and scholarly matters. He tells Martha that Mary has chosen "the better part." Mary has chosen "the one thing that is essential. She has chosen the main course." Mary has chosen the incarnate word of God. She has opted to get out of the kitchen and sit at the feet of Jesus.

Jesus was not just any ordinary man to whom Mary and Martha paid homage. He was more than ordinary; he was their Lord. In John 11 Mary and Martha addressed Jesus as Lord when they asked him for help with Lazarus. Even though the visit to Martha and Mary recorded in our Lukan text preceded the raising of Lazarus from the dead and the anointing of Jesus, they regarded Jesus as Lord, an authority figure, a rabbi, and a prophet. While both sisters accepted Jesus as Lord, the text says that Mary was the only one who sat at his feet.

Martha was distracted by the exquisite preparations she was making in the kitchen. She was very annoyed with her sister Mary's absence from the kitchen. Perhaps Martha was concerned for Mary's reputation. Impulsively and boldly Mary had forsaken the pots and pans in the kitchen to sit at the feet of Jesus. Did she not know that such a privilege was reserved for men only? Had Mary lost touch with her cultural reality? Martha may have wondered to herself what people would say about her sister taking on a male role in a patriarchal society.

Martha may have been merely anxious about the fact that there was so much work to do in the kitchen to get dinner ready for their house guests. She might have felt abandoned by Mary. Maybe she thought to herself, "Why do I have to do all the 'grunt work' by myself?" Maybe she felt overwhelmed by preparing for Jesus and his disciples. She had been accustomed to cooking for a few people. Now she had extra people to accommodate. In my sanctified imagination I can hear Martha saying to Jesus, "this isn't fair, Jesus. Make Mary come back into the kitchen and help me! Don't you care that I am in here working like a slave, all by myself?"

Jesus empathized with Martha and felt her pain. But he replied, "Martha dear, you are anxious about many things. Mary has chosen the better part; I am not going to take that away from her." While the text ends at this point and closes Dr. Luke's tenth chapter, I believe that Jesus likely had more to say to Martha. I imagine he said, "Sister-girl, take a break from all that busy work you are doing. Get out of the kitchen! Come over here and sit down for a little while. We can eat dinner later. Besides, the main course is over here with me. Your sister has the right idea." Taste and see that the Lord is good.

Mary chose the better part. I am glad she had the courage to break with tradition. I am grateful that Jesus supported her bold move toward cultural emancipation. Mary's story reminds me of my own story. I never had the opportunity to grow up in my father's house as a child. That's another story. But as a young teenager I had occasion to visit him in his home on special days. Family members and friends would come to my father's house for Sunday dinners and fellowship. My father, a longshoreman, along with several of his brothers worked on the Baltimore waterfront. They shared interesting and adventuresome stories about life on the waterfront sitting in the living room of my Dad's house. I loved to sit on a stool at the foot of my Dad's chair and listen to the stories that were told by him, my uncles, and my father's friends. My Dad welcomed me sitting on a stool next to him. Rarely did I spend much time in the kitchen on those special days. It seemed to me, then, that the men had the better part. The women who stayed in the kitchen cooking the meal had the hardest job. The men just sat around telling each other stories until dinner was ready to be served. When dinner was ready, they invariably, were served first. My ambivalence about Mary's place of privilege becomes apparent, because I can also empathize and relate to Martha. Martha, along with many other women, has been in the kitchen, working feverishly among the pots and pans preparing soul food for the heart. Every time I dine at the Culinary School of Arts restaurant in Birmingham, Alabama I am reminded that somebody has to do the cooking and that cooking is hard work. It is an art which requires love, skill, commitment of time and energy. And when the gourmet meal is prepared to perfection, it will make you forget your manners and sing at the dinner table. Martha most likely felt overwhelmed by the demands that were being placed on her. She was in the kitchen, but the main course was in another room.

The Bible says that Mary chose "the better part." The better part or "main course" is the word of God. The one thing that is necessary for both women and men is the Word. Both men and women have access to the "main course." Both women and men can sit at the feet of Jesus and be his disciples. Loving God and loving our neighbor ought to be our entree of choice. Sometimes the "main course" requires us to break with traditional fare to try something different.

In both the story of the Samaritan which precedes the story of Mary and Martha, and the story in our text there is a break with conventional tradition and cultural practices. Mary exemplifies the fulfillment of the first commandment, "you are to love the Lord your God with all your heart, with all your soul, and with all your energy, and with your mind." While the Samaritan story speaks to the second commandment, "you are to love your neighbor as yourself."[12]

What can we learn from the story of Mary and Martha that will help us and the church to put our priorities in order? We need to make sitting at the feet of Jesus and listening to his word our first priority. The church must take the responsibility to provide us with trained clergy who can take us to the deep well of intimacy with Christ. No longer is hamburger helper or somebody's else's leftovers satisfactory to reach the un-churched who have been educated in the ivory halls of the academy, read more than their preachers and who have grown accustomed to prime rib, filet mignon, and fried lobster. Educated people deserve a gourmet meal to satisfy their hungry hearts. It is time for the church to get out of the kitchen and spend some quality time with Jesus. And for some of our fearless leaders this means going back to school, or going on a retreat or a sabbatical to become reacquainted with the presence and power of the Holy Spirit.

We live in an era and a society where Alvin Toffler's *Future Shock* is no longer future but a present reality. Twenty-first century technology has placed us on the super information highway. In order to keep up churches have created more ministries to maintain a competitive edge. Too much precious time is spent meeting in the kitchen to plan the next meeting. We have become so distracted by the activities of having church that we have neglected the "one essential thing." We must put first things first. We must retreat from the madness of being busy just to be busy and spend quality time with Jesus. We must reclaim the spiritual discipline of contemplative listening. We must listen to the heart of God so that we may know, love, and experience him where he is at work. In order for this to become a reality in our lives we must take time off and get out of the kitchen. The church can not afford to spend too much energy and time in the kitchen frying chicken, making potato salad, baking bread, and making Kool-Aid. These are the non-essentials.

The Bible says that the Kingdom of God is not meat nor

drink but righteousness, peace, and joy in the Holy Ghost.[13] Our sensibilities have become distracted by the fragrant aromas of the biscuits and rolls baking in the oven. We have lost sight of the "main course." Jesus speaks to the church today. He reminds us in his own words, "I am the bread of life. He who comes to me will never go hungry, and he who believes in me will never be thirsty." The church needs to refocus. We don't need more Kool-Aid, but we do need the Jesus who can turn water into wine.[14]

Now is the time for the church to be bold and impulsive like Mary. It is time for the church to break out of the bondage of cultural traditions. It is time for the church to sit at the feet of Jesus and hang on his every word. Then and only then will we begin to see true transformation in the lives of people and our communities.

3 | Do Your Part

"Some men came, bringing to him a paralytic, carried by four of them. Since they could not get him to Jesus because of the crowd, they made an opening in the roof above Jesus and after digging through it, lowered the mat the paralyzed man was lying on."

(Mark 2:3–4, NIV)

The illegal drug market is creating chaos in our communities, and it is systematically stripping our families of their self-worth. Not only is the drug trafficking creating chaos in our neighborhoods and robbing families of their self-esteem, but it is also paralyzing our young people. The drug trade is producing a generation of impotent, unconscious citizens. King Heroine, Queen Mother, Crack Cocaine, and Prince Oxycotin have formed an unholy alliance. They have manipulated a host of unenlightened, spiritually depressed, and marginalized people into believing that

15

they are the best thing that ever happened to them.

As a result of the infiltration of drugs into our villages, nursing homes are witnessing a significant increase in their admission roles. No longer is it just our traditional, disabled, elderly saints inhabiting these assisted living facilities, but now there is an influx of young African American males and females who occupy rooms in nursing homes. Many of these young adults have moved to nursing homes, because they are paralyzed. Some of them have been paralyzed by drug related gunshot wounds. Others of them have found a home in residential institutions, because they have had a midnight rendezvous with AIDS.

It is a terrible thing to be addicted to drugs. Drug addiction will make you steal from your neighbor, your brother, your sister, your mother and your father. Drug addiction will make you prostitute yourself before false gods. Drugs will make you neglect your job, your church, your children, and yourself. Drug addiction is no respecter of persons. It is an equal opportunity oppressor.

When drugs call your name, they don't care about your skin color, your gender, your sexual orientation, your educational level or your socioeconomic status. It doesn't matter whether you are an athlete, doctor, lawyer, bishop, preacher, teacher, or a high school drop-out. Anybody can become a member of the Drug Addiction Society. You don't have to pledge, you don't have to go on line, and you don't have to beg to be included. All you have to do is take a hit. Snort up some cocaine or shoot up some heroine, and you can quickly become a dues paying member in good and regular standing of the "don't bother me; I can't cope" crowd.[15]

Beloved, no longer can Christians, afford to drive by open air drug markets in many of our major cities on Sunday mornings to comfortable sanctuaries and say, "what a shame, look at the drug addicts milling around like ants on the street corner waiting for the candy man." No, beloved, I just stopped by to tell you that you have to do your part to clean up the streets and make a difference in the lives of those persons who are crippled by their addictions.

If the truth be told, many of us are crippled by our addiction to something. Your addiction might not be drugs, but it is something. It might not be alcohol, but it is something. It might not be food, but it is something. It might not be sex, but it is something. It might not be a critical attitude, but it is something. It might not be an abusive relationship, but it is something. It might not be materialism, but it is something. I don't know what has crippled you and hampered your ability to get out of your negative life style, but I do know someone who can pick you up, turn you around and plant your feet on solid ground.

In our text, Mark 2:1–12 we find the story of some men who helped another "brother" move from Paralysis Avenue to Restoration Drive. This story is instructive for us in that it shows us that we need to do our part. Tradition has it that the gospel of Mark was written after the death of Peter (A.D. 64) at least 35 years after the events described. This seems to suggest that the writer did not personally participate in the events narrated in this gospel, but wrote about what he had heard from others.[16] Some scholars suggest that this book may have been written during the persecution of Christians under the rule of Nero (64–68 A.D.)

Mark wrote this book to encourage his fellow comrades on their Christian journey. He wrote this gospel during a period when the fledgling church was in crisis and transition. It was in crisis, because of the horrific persecutions, and it was in transition, because of its move from its original home in the Semitic culture of Palestinian Judaism to the Gentile culture of the Roman Empire.[17] This transition brought about tension between those who espoused the traditional Jewish customs and those who favored the freedom of the new Gentile Christianity. It was against this sociological and historical backdrop that Mark presents Jesus from the revolutionary perspective of the new Gentile Christianity.

17

Let's look closely at the story. As a matter of fact, let's go inside the story. Imagine yourself being one of the four men. You have decided to help an incapacitated brother get to Jesus. Or if you are not timid, imagine that you are the one who is paralyzed, trapped, and unable to walk to reach Jesus. Pause and reflect for a moment. Allow yourself to be with what ever role you feel comfortable. This is not only the story of a paralyzed man, but it is also our story to the extent that we allow ourselves to become a part of the text.

The scene opens with us in a town called Capernaum. We know from Mark 2:1 that Jesus enters Capernaum and goes home. Capernaum offered Jesus two distinct advantages. First, it was a crossroad of primary importance. It was a border town situated along the main imperial highway leading to Damascus. Second, Capernaum was far enough away from the big centers such as Tiberius where Herod Antipas set up his capitol. Furthermore, the population of Capernaum was diverse: fishermen, farmers, artists, merchants, publicans and others lived in the same village. There was seemingly no economic inequality. Relations between the citizens of Capernaum and the Romans were cordial. For the most part all the people living in Capernaum were hard workers, extremely frugal and open-minded. This is the town where Jesus made his home.

It was Peter's house that became the "house of Jesus." Peter's house was situated 30 miles south of the synagogue. It was a large house which consisted of several roofed-rooms, clustering around a courtyard. This house was so spacious that the gospels tell us three families, the families of Peter, his brother Andrew, and Peter's mother-in-law lived together in this one house.[18] People gathered in the house and outside in the front of the door to hear Jesus. Those who couldn't get in the house or near the front door filled up the courtyard.

We were there. Don't you remember the day when Jesus was teaching and four men tried to bring a paralyzed man into the house? I remember as though it were yesterday, because there were a lot of good-looking men in the house. It is quite probable that these four were fishermen with big hearts who were determined to help a brother. They carried the crippled man to the courtyard of the house. There were so many people standing around the front door listening to Jesus. It was tight. But then I saw the four men circumvent the crowd and take the stone steps to the roof. At first I could not believe my eyes. Why would they take a paralyzed man to the roof?

The roof was made of wooden beams and of beaten earth mixed with straw.[19] I watched them from among the crowd as they passionately pulled apart the beams from the straw. I saw them lift the mat with the paralytic down through the rooftop into the center of the room where Jesus was teaching. The Bible says, "When Jesus saw their faith, he said to the paralytic, son, your sins are forgiven." (Mark 2:5)

Jesus met the paralytic at his greatest level of need. The man was broken, had sinned and needed forgiveness. Jesus offers him forgiveness. I don't know whether his personal sins caused him to be paralyzed. I don't know whether he got caught in the crossfire of a back alley fight in Capernaum. But I do know that Jesus forgave him.

There were some naysayers in the crowd as might be expected who observed Jesus with critical intentions. They asked Jesus to explain how it was that he could forgive sins. They accused him of blasphemy. "Who can forgive sins but God alone?" (Mark 2:7b) Jesus knew immediately what they were thinking. And He said to them, "Which is easier to say to the paralytic, 'Your sins are forgiven,' or to say, 'Get up take your mat and walk.'" But that you may know that the Son of man has authority on earth to forgive sins ... he said to the man "get up, take your mat and walk home." (Mark 2:9–10) The man picked up his mat and walked out of the room so that everybody could see him.

What might we learn from this story that will help us deal with our modern day paralytics? Drugs have crippled many of our brothers and sisters. What can we do? Whatever you can do, do your part. God wants to use us to make a difference in the lives of women and men who are stuck in their addictions. We can be fearless, persistent Christians and carry the psychologically and spiritually crippled to the house of Jesus. We can break through the rooftops of the traditional established order. Do your part to help the addict get a front seat at the altar of life. There is forgiveness, healing, and deliverance at the feet of Jesus.

What else might we glean from this passage? The Bible says, "Some men came, bringing to him a paralytic, carried by four of them ..." This suggests to me that we ought not to go alone to rescue the perishing.[20] We need to take others with us who are strong in the faith to bear witness and help us carry the load. The devil is busy going about like a roaring lion seeking whom he may devour. It is always good to have brothers and or sisters to accompany you on the journey. Together we will be able to withstand the wiles of the devil.

Do your part to get the modern day paralytics into a safe-house called church where they can bloom in the *koinonia* (fellowship) of the saints. It is in the safety of the rooms that addicts can make contact with Jesus and say:

"We admitted we were powerless over our addictions, that our lives had become unmanageable, came to believe that a power greater than ourselves could restore us to sanity, made a decision to turn our will and our lives over to the care of God as we understood Him ..."

My friend, Bishop John R. Bryant and former pastor of Bethel AME Church, Baltimore, Maryland recognized the need for the church to be a safe haven for contemporary paralytics. It was under his preaching and compassionate acceptance that Tabitha Anonymous, a former drug addict, moved from crippling drug addiction to abstinence and sanity. Tabitha came to church "high" on a regular basis before she finally yielded to the work of the Holy Spirit. One day Tabitha heard Rev. Bryant say, "For God so loved the world that He gave his only begotten son that whosoever believes in Him should not perish but have everlasting life." (John 3:16) She threw her drugs down at the altar. Tabitha with the support of her church family founded the Freedom Now Ministry, a ministry for recovering addicts. It is no secret what God can do.

"Which is easier to say to the paralytic, 'your sins are forgiven,' or to say, 'get up, take your mat and walk?'" (Mark 2:9) Do your part and Jesus will do the rest.

4 | You've Got the Power

"But you will receive power when the Holy Spirit comes on you; and you will be my witnesses in Jerusalem, and in all Judea and Samaria, and to the ends of the earth."
(Acts 1:8, NIV)

There was a power shortage in Jerusalem. A cloud of darkness hovered over the city. The one Bright Light had gone out. A major travesty of justice had taken place. The Chief Engineer and servant of the newly emerging G&N Power Plant, the Good News Power Plant, had been assassinated by terrorists. Much of the leadership of the Good News Power Plant had scattered and had run for cover. They ran, because they were afraid of what might happen to them.

Some of the G&N workers had watched from afar as the terrorist publicly humiliated and ridiculed the Chief Engineer. They watched from afar as the terrorists stripped him and beat him with leather whips. They watched from afar as he dragged an old rugged cross on his shoulders. They watched from afar as he fell down three times. They watched as his enemies hung him high and stretched him wide. They watched as he gave up the ghost and died. Darkness came over the earth in the middle of the day when the Chief Engineer died. Even the veil of the temple was split in half. It was a dark season in Jerusalem.

Many of the workers of the G&N Power Plant went into hiding, while the company scrambled to reorganize. The workers were confused, fatigued, and disoriented. They seemed to be suffering from depression and post traumatic stress disorder. They lacked energy, and they had no power. They forgot that the Chief Engineer had warned them about his pending death. He had promised to comfort them with the promise of a Counselor. He even told them that he would rise again.

Ben Satan, the mastermind behind the plot to kill the Chief Engineer, thought he had the victory over the Good News Power Plant when the Chief Engineer died. But the Chief Engineer did not stay in the tomb. As a matter of fact *The Jerusalem Times* reported that he got up with all power in his hands. However, the story does not end there. Yes, the Chief Engineer got up and because he got and the Holy Ghost got up with him; I just stopped by to tell you that you've got the power.

Read with me, if you please, Acts 1:1–11. In this biblical text we discover that Dr. Luke, a physician by trade and a prolific writer by destiny sent a copy of his manuscript to his publisher and financial backer, Theophilus. He reminds Theophilus of what he previously wrote about in his first book, *Luke*. The gospel writer says I wrote about all that Jesus did. I told you about his birth, how he was born of a virgin and conceived by the Holy Ghost. (Luke 1:34–35) I told you about the time he was twelve years old and was left behind in Jerusalem by his parents.[21] I told you about his baptism and genealogy. I told you how he grew into

24

manhood and was tempted by the devil for forty days.[22] I told you how he was rejected in his home town.[23] I even told you about his betrayal, death, and resurrection.[24] And I told you about his glorious ascension into heaven, but now, Theophilus, in this book, my second book, *Acts*, I am going to tell you about the power of the Holy Ghost.[25]

I want you to visualize Theophilus writing a response to Dr. Luke with his editorial comments:

> Luke my friend, I am a lover of God. I know about God the Father, the creator of the heavens and the earth. I know about Jesus the Christ who thought it not robbery to wrap himself up in human flesh and to become like us in everything accept sin. But I must confess to you, my brother, that I need a little clarification on the Holy Ghost. Who is the Holy Ghost? And why do you believe in the Holy Ghost?

Dr. Luke, in turn, writes back to Theophilus saying:

> I am glad you asked about the Holy Ghost. Our God is one, Theophilus.[26] The Holy Ghost is God Almighty, the third person in the Holy Trinity. He was in the beginning before there was a beginning, and he will be with us until the end, even after time ceases to exist. The Holy Ghost is synonymous with the Holy Spirit. Old Testament writers refer to him as the *Ruah*, the spirit of the Lord (Isaiah 63: 10) and in the Greek New Testament as the *Pneuma*, the breath of the Lord. The Holy Ghost is generally an expression for God's power; the extension of himself, whereby he carries out many of his deeds.[27] The role of the Holy Ghost in the Old Testament is as the spirit of prophecy.

The prophet Joel talked about the Holy Ghost in his book. Joel had a private interview with God. God told Joel to tell the people that *in the latter days I will pour out my spirit on all people. Your sons and daughters will prophesy, your young men will see visions, your old men will dream dreams. Even on my servants, both men and women, I will pour out my spirit in those days, and they will prophesy.* (Joel 2:28–32)

Jesus who is the foundation for the *New Testament* understood the Holy Ghost as a personality.[28] Jesus gathered with the disciples for the Passover before he went to the cross. He told the disciples that he was going away, but that he would not leave them without a Comforter. Jesus said, "And I will pray to the Father, and he will give you another Comforter (one of the same kind), that he may abide with you forever." Jesus was referring to the *Paracletos*, the Holy Spirit. The Paraclete, Counselor or Advocate would come along side the disciples and guide them into all truth. (John 16:13)

Jesus told his disciples to stay in Jerusalem and to wait for the promise of the Father. He said, John baptized with water, but you shall be baptized with the Holy Ghost not many days hence. They wanted to know if Jesus was going to restore the kingdom of Israel. Jesus told them not to worry about that, but they would receive power, miraculous power, wonder working power, after the Holy Ghost is come upon them.[29] And they would be witnesses unto him in Jerusalem and in all Judea, and in Samaria and unto the uttermost part of the earth.

Using creative literary license Luke might have continued his reply to Theophilus by saying: man its simple for me. I believe in the Holy Ghost, because the prophets of old foreshadowed him and Jesus Christ said it was so. Not only that but if you read my second chapter, you will find that when the day of Pentecost was fully come they were all with one accord in one place. They had been praying for ten days. Suddenly there came a sound as a rushing mighty wind, and it filled the house. There appeared tongues of fire which sat on each persons head, and they were all filled with the Holy Ghost.

They began to speak in diverse tongues, and everybody from every nation understood what they were saying in their own language. They made so much noise and commotion that some of the onlookers thought they were drunk. But they were not drunk, because it was too early in the day. They were filled with the Holy Ghost.

And not only did they receive the gift of the outpouring of the Holy Ghost, but if you read verses 38–39 of my second chapter in Acts you will discover that the promise of the Holy Ghost was not limited to them. The promise is unto you and your children, and to all that are afar off, even as many as the Lord shall call.

My brothers and my sisters, even though there appears to be a power shortage in the global community, you've got the power to turn the lights back on. If you believe in the Lord Jesus Christ and have accepted him as your Lord and Savior, then you've got the power. You've got the Father, the Son, and the Holy Ghost. You've got the power to teach all nations. You've got the power to go to Israel, Jordan, Palestine, and Afghanistan. You've got the power to go to Barbados, Guyana, Jamaica, and Haiti. You've got the power to go to Russia, Saudi Arabia and Iran. You've got the power to go to the uttermost part of the earth and witness for the cause of Jesus Christ.

Not only do you have the power to go overseas and witness but you have the power to step out of the box and stretch your boundaries in the United States of America. Our nation is weeping, because the lights have gone out in New York City, Los Angeles,

Philadelphia, and Washington, D.C. You've got the power to be a balm in Gilead. I don't know about you, but I believe in the Holy Ghost.

The Holy Ghost is like fire shut up in my bones. He puts clapping in my hands, running in my feet, shouting in my spirit, and joy in my heart. If you believe in the Holy Ghost, then know this one thing, you've got the power!

5 | Your Will Be Done

"This, then, is how you should pray: Our Father in heaven, hallowed be your name, your kingdom come, your will be done on earth as it is in heaven."
(Matthew 6:9–10, NIV)

The global community is confronting a potentially, cataclysmic crisis of cosmic proportions. Not only is terrorism sending shock waves of trepidation around the American homeland, but terrorism is also rearing its ugly head in Bali, Kenya, Israel, and Palestine. At the same time the silent terror—AIDS is finally recognized by the Chinese government as a life threatening reality with over one million reported cases not withstanding the millions of Africans, and African-American women and men who are HIV compromised.

We are standing at the crossroads of secularism, humanism, militarism, and Christianity. Secularism declares that there is no

God. Therefore, we should eat, drink, and be merry, because what you see is what you get. Humanism says that if it feels good do it, because "I'm okay and you're okay." Militarism threatens humanity with weapons of mass destruction and promotes an ideology of "vengeance is mine." Christianity, on the other hand, cries out from the depths of its crucified heart in the garden of Gethsemane, "your will be done."

As you consider the theme, "Doing God's will, God's way," I want to direct your attention to our subject for this discourse: "Your Will Be Done." In the text also found in Luke 11:1–2 we find these words:

"And it came to pass, that as he was praying in a certain place, when he ceased, one of his disciples said unto him, Lord teach us to pray, as John also taught his disciples. And he said unto them. When ye pray, say, Our Father which art in heaven, Hallowed be thy name. Thy Kingdom come, Thy will be done, as in heaven, so on earth."[30]

One of Jesus' disciples made what seemed to be a simple, uncomplicated request. "Lord, teach us to pray." Are we to assume that these men did not know how to pray? A closer look at the background of these Jewish men will reveal that they already knew how to pray. We only have to look to Jesus and his Jewish cultural context to discover that these men were knowledgeable in the Torah. Jesus was reared in a devout Jewish home where prayer was customary. We know that praying was a daily part of the Jewish males practice. We know that by New Testament times the custom of praying three times a day was the general rule. (Acts 3:1, 10: 3, 30) We know that it was the minimum of religious practices to recite the *Shema*, the creed, twice a day, "Hear, O Israel: the Lord our God is one God." (Deuteronomy 6:4). Jewish men also prayed the *Tephilla* [a hymn of benediction.][31]

We also know that the custom of praying three times a day was testified to by Daniel in the Old Testament. Daniel had windows in his upper room which opened in the direction of Jerusalem. He would kneel three times a day to pray and praise God. (Daniel 6:11)

It wasn't that the disciples did not know how to pray. They were devout Jews. Surely they knew how to pray. They had been praying the required prayers three times a day since the age of twelve, their Bar Mitzvah or rite of passage. Of course the disciples knew how to pray, but they wanted something more. They wanted their own special prayer.

Sisters and brothers, whenever folks join a sorority, fraternity, or Masonic lodge, they want their own song, their own step, their own motto, their own colors, and their own creed. The disciples were no different. They wanted their own unique prayer which would distinguish them from their other Jewish brothers. They wanted people to know that they were followers of a new way. "Lord, teach us to pray" is to say, "Give us our own prayer."

Jesus says when you pray, "pray like this. Our Father which art in heaven, hallowed be thy name. Thy kingdom come, thy will be done." Pray "our Father," because the Father is the creator of all humanity. Pray with the fellowship of the believers in mind. Pray, "hallowed be your name," because God's name is holy. And pray "thy will be done."

To pray "your will be done" is to say, "I want to do God's will, God's way." This is often hard to do, because walking in this declaration is what separates the real Disciples of Christ from the "want to bees." To pray "your will be done" is to comprehend the profundity of the imperative. It is no longer my will and my way, but it is God's will and God's way. I yield to God's gracious and sovereign purpose for my life. I request the kingdom of God to come in its fullness and to come now.

When we pray, "thy will be done," we are asking to be broken. When I was a youngster, I would accompany my mother to Pimlico Race Track in Baltimore City to watch the horse races.

31

I learned from an early age that the horses had to be broken in order to become good horses for racing. They had to learn how to obey the commands of their jockey and trainer. Occasionally, when the jockey would approach the starting gate, a horse might buck, pull backward, and refuse to go into the gate. Many times I have observed the jockey whip the horse in order to get the horse to go where he wanted her to go. When we pray, "your will be done," we may well be asking for a whipping from the Master Trainer. But if we want to cross the finish line, we have to say yes to his will and yes to his way.

When we pray, "thy will be done," not only are we asking to be broken, but we are reaffirming our Christian confession that Jesus is Lord of our lives. We declare that we belong to the Society of Jesus. We pledge our allegiance to Jesus, not Osama Ben Laden, not to Mohammed, not to Buddha, not to Amen Ra, and not to Wall Street. But as the called out of Christ we pledge allegiance to Christ, the anointed one, the Alpha and the Omega, the Beginning and the End, the King of kings, and the Lord of lords.

Lastly, beloved when we pray, "thy will be done," we may be asking God to give us a "cave experience." What do you mean by that preacher? I am glad you asked. Sometimes we have to retreat to a cave in order to hear clearly what God's will is for our lives.

Charles Spurgeon, a 19th century preacher put it this way:

Have none of you ever noticed, in your own lives, that
whenever God is going to give you an enlargement, and
bring you out to a larger sphere of service, or a higher
platform of spiritual life, you always get thrown down?
That is his usual way of working ... He strips you before
he robs you ... David is to be king in Jerusalem, but he
must go to the throne by wave of the cave. Now, are any of
you here going to heaven, or going to a more heavenly state

of sanctification, or going to a greater sphere of usefulness: Do not wonder if you go by the way of the cave.[32]

"Your will be done" is a prayer that will break us, shape us, and mold us to conform to God's will and God's way. Jesus went to the Garden of Gethsemane for his cave experience. He prayed so earnestly that his sweat became like drops of blood. He knelt down and prayed, "Father if thou be willing, remove this cup from me: nevertheless not my will, but thy will be done." Jesus yielded his will to his father's will and made the ultimate sacrifice. It was at the cross. Jesus submitted and completed his father's will.

We have some challenging days ahead of us. The world is in turmoil. There are wars and rumors of wars. AIDS has reached pandemic proportions, leaving millions of children orphaned. Secularism, humanism, and militarism are trying to run the red light and push themselves through the crossroads of life over against Christianity. What are we to do?

Is there anybody here who wants to do God's will, God's way? Is there anybody here who will say, "your will be done?" Are you willing to be broken for the sake of Christ and his Kingdom, to do what God says do and to go where he leads you? If you are willing to do God's will, God's way then say, "yes, Lord! All to Jesus I surrender. All to him I freely give. I will ever love and trust him. In his presence daily live. I surrender all; I surrender all. All to thee my blessed Savior, I surrender all."[33]

6 | Lead Us Not Into Temptation

One day Jesus was praying in a certain place. When he finished, one of his disciples said to him, Lord, teach us to pray, just as John taught his disciples. He said to them, "when you pray, say: 'Father hallowed be your name, your kingdom come. Give us each day our daily bread. Forgive us our sins, for we also forgive everyone who sins against us. And lead us not into temptation.'"

(Luke 11:1–4, NIV)

Life is pregnant with temptation. The international community is confronting a cataclysmic temptation of cosmic proportions. Terrorism is sending shock waves of fear around the world. Man's inhumanity to humanity, throughout the world, under the guise of religious fanaticism is fostering a spirit of despair and powerlessness. In the midst of trauma, shock, and hopelessness still small

35

voices cry out from the depths of their souls, "lead us not into temptation."

As we peruse the perimeter of our text today, we want to zoom our sermonic spotlight onto Luke 11:4b. There we will find these words in the New International Version of the Bible: "And lead us not into temptation." For the time that is allowed me this morning I want to tag this text for preaching: Lead Us Not into Temptation.

Life is full of temptation. The sagacious professor of systematic theology, Jan Lockman says, "For each and every day our whole life is exposed to temptation and assault."[34] Life is full of temptation, because Adam and Eve made a fatal mistake in the Garden of Eden when they decided to disobey God. As a result of their original sin pain, suffering, stress, disappointment, and death have become the plight of all humankind. Life is pregnant with temptation and we are inclined towards sin from birth. We often yield to the negative thoughts of our imaginations.

David, a man after God's on heart, understood temptation. He had to have Bathsheba, so he sent her husband, Uriah, to the front line of the battle field in order to get rid of him. That's why David could pray so passionately, "Create in me a clean heart, O God; and renew a right spirit within me."[35]

Augustine, the Bishop of Hippo, was familiar with temptation. He admits in his Confessions that before he got converted, he had a son, *Adeodatus*, out of wedlock, by his lover of many years. That's why he could fervently pray to God his prayer of conversion: "late have I loved you, o Beauty ever ancient, ever new, late have I loved you! ... You called, you shouted and you broke through my deafness."

Martin Luther understood this phenomenon better than most. Temptation was a key word in his life and his theology. Luther understood how critically important it was for the believer to pray, everyday, "lead us not into temptation."

Jesus was led by the Spirit in the wilderness being tested by the devil for forty days, but he did not yield to the temptation.[36] He could have come down from the cross just to save himself, but he decided to stay there for you and me.

As a child I recall hearing my mother who graduated from the school of hard knocks with an eighth grade education and served in a segregated U.S. Women's Auxiliary Corp during World War II say, "Patricia, in this life you will have trials and tribulations. The grass always looks greener on the other side. You are going to have some temptations in life, but be good child. Get an education. Make something of yourself. Life is full of temptation."

When we pray, lead us not into temptation, we need to understand the profundity of what we are saying. Before we pray, and lead us not into temptation, we have already asked for the Kingdom to come; we have asked for God's will to be done; we have asked for enough bread for today; we have asked the Father to forgive us our debts as we forgive those who trespass against us. Then we come to the conjunction, "and." In my old neighborhood, Sandtown, growing up in inner city Baltimore, we used to say, "The function is at the junction." But in this pericope the function is at the conjunction. In both the Lukan version of the Lord's Prayer and the Matthean version the "sixth petition, like the fifth before it, is introduced with the conjunction 'and.' The use of 'and' indicates that the petition stands in some continuity with the one that precedes it."[37]

When we pray " and lead us not into temptation," Joachim Jeremias points out that this petition "departs from the pattern of the previous petitions in that it is the only one formulated in the negative. But all that is intentional; as the contents show, this petition is supposed to stand out as harsh and abrupt."[38]

At first glance the text, lead us not into temptation, seems to suggest that God is the one who leads us into temptation. But this is certainly contrary to what James writes in his epistle. James

says, "Let no one say when he is tempted, 'I am tempted by God';
for God cannot be tempted with evil, and he himself tempts no
one."[39] In this circumstance the word temptation does not capture
the full meaning or depth of this concluding petition. According to
Jeremias the Greek word *peirasmos* can have two meanings: "(1)
temptation, i.e., being mislead into sin, and (2) trial or testing, i.e.
faith or fidelity being put to the test."[40] The final petition has to
do with the testing of the faith. This petition has very little to do
with the everyday temptations of life, but rather the final testing
of our faith. This last petition addresses the ultimate temptation
which is the eschatological temptation. What is the eschatological
temptation, preacher? I'm glad you asked.

The eschatological temptation has to do with the testing that
will precede the Last Judgment. When we pray, "and lead us not
into temptation," we are asking not to be spared temptation, but
that God will help us to overcome temptation. We pray that God
will help us overcome the final great temptation which will be revealed to the whole world. The eschatological temptation or final
testing is the temptation of apostasy. To yield to the temptation of
apostasy means to turn your back on your faith in Jesus Christ.
When we pray, "And lead us not into temptation," we are saying
to God even if it means martyrdom for the sake of Christ, help us
to overcome the temptation to deny our belief in Jesus.

The Bible says in the book of Revelation that souls had been
beheaded, because of their testimony for Jesus, and because of the
word of God. They had not worshipped the beast or his image
and had not received his mark on their foreheads. They came to
life and reigned with Christ a thousand years.[41]

Life is full of temptations. We live in a society where sexual im-
morality, pornography, and sexual abuse of children by clergy are
running rampant in and out of the closet. We live in an era where
there are wars and rumors of wars. Nations are rising up against
nations and kingdoms are rising up against kingdoms. Christians

are being persecuted and put to death in India, Iraq, Guatemala, Pakistan, Russia, and Yemen. People are turning away from the faith, while false prophets are deceiving the masses of people. When we pray, and lead us not into temptation, we are praying to the Father to preserve us from turning our backs on Jesus Christ. When the final testing comes, we will need the strength and power of the Holy Spirit, we will need the grace and mercy of Jesus to get us across the finish line. On our own strength we can do nothing, because the enemy is like a roaring lion going about seeking whom he may devour.

When I was in junior high school, I used to run track in the junior Olympics. My coach, Mr. Lampkin would tell us to keep our eye beyond the finish line. He said that the goal was to cross the finish line no matter what. Even if we got tired, or experienced muscle pain, we were to press our way across the finish line. It wasn't enough to get to the finish line and stop short, but we had to cross the finish line. Mr. Lampkin would say, "When you see the finish line in sight, stay focused and don't look back. If you look back, you will get distracted and throw your pace off." He said, "Pray for that extra kick and run as fast as you can across the finish line." When we pray, and lead us not into temptation, we are asking God to help us stay focused on Jesus, to give us that extra Holy Ghost kick, to keep our eye on the Prize, and to help us make it across the finish line of our faith.

Can I get a witness? I hear Brother Paul saying: "Not that I have already obtained all this, or have already been made perfect, but I press on to take hold of that for which Christ Jesus took hold of me. Brothers (*and Sisters*) I do not consider myself yet to have taken hold of it. But one thing I do; forgetting what is behind and straining toward what is ahead, I press on toward the goal to win the prize for which God has called me heavenward in Christ Jesus."[42]

What can we glean from this text today that will help us deal with the temptation to turn our back on Jesus and deny the faith?

Life is pregnant with temptation. We need to be vigilant and prayerful so that we will yield not to temptation. We must keep our sights on crossing the finish line. We don't want to stop short of our goal which is eternal life. And so my brothers and my sisters, our daily prayer must be, "lead us not into temptation."

From this text Dr. Luke would have us to understand that when the midnight of our lives comes, and it will come and temptation is calling our name and is knocking at our door, we must come before the throne of Grace to our Father with holy boldness and ask God for what we need.

Luke says, "ask and it will be given to you; seek and you will find, knock and the door will be opened."[43] If, then, we who are sinners know how to give good gifts to our children, certainly our Father who art in Heaven will give us the Holy Ghost if we ask Him.[44]

Beloved, I can see the other side of the finish line in front of me. I won't look back, I won't step back, and I won't go back. I'm pressing my way. I don't feel "no" ways tired. Jesus brought me too far to leave me. Lord, give me that extra kick.

> I see a new heaven and a new earth, for the first heaven
> and the first earth have passed away and there is no longer
> any sea. I see the Holy City, New Jerusalem, coming down
> out of heaven from God, prepared as a bride beautifully
> dressed for her husband. And I hear a loud voice from the
> throne saying, now the dwelling of God is with men and
> he will live with them. You will be my people, and I will
> be your God. There will be no more weeping and wailing.
> There will be no more death, or mourning, no more good-
> byes for the old order of things has passed away.[45]

I don't know about you, but I want to cross the finish line. Is there anybody else who wants to cross the finish line? If so, you ought to stand on your feet all over the chapel, give God the glory, give God the praise. Take your mark, get set, and get ready to run the race with faith. And when you see the finish line in sight, ask God to let the Holy Ghost fall fresh upon you so that you will:

Yield not to temptation. For yielding is sin; each victory will help you some other To win; fight manfully onward, dark passions subdue. Look ever to Jesus, He'll carry you through. Ask the Savior to help you, comfort, strengthen, and keep you; He is willing to aid you, He will carry you through.[46]

7 | Call Me by My Name

"Repent, then, and turn to God, so that times of refreshing may come from the Lord, and that he may send the Christ, who has been appointed for you—even Jesus."
(Acts 3:19–20,NIV)

I can't rap like Sista Soldier, or sing like Erica Badu or Pattie Labelle. I can't write like Maya Angelou or Renita Weems; I can't talk like Oprah Winfrey or preach like Vashti McKenzie, but God told me that I can express myself, so He commissioned me to write a poem a few weeks ago. If you will indulge me a few moments, I will use my poem to introduce this sermon:

What's your name?
Make him call you by your name.
There's something special about your name.
Make him call you by your name.

Don't play the anon-y-mous game.
Make him call you by your name.
What's your name?
African Queen, Royal ambassador of the most high—
    God.
What's your name?
African Queen, Royal ambassador of the most high—
    God.
Your name is Akosua, Cecelia, Geneva Marie.
Your name is Esther, Thema Simone, Patricia Anne,
What's your name?
Your name is Letitia, Janie Mc, Paulette and Ruth.
Make him call you by your name.
What's your name?
Your name is Vashti, Victoria, and Veronica, too.
What's your name?
Your name is Beautiful One,
Made in the Image and the likeness of God.
Your name is Steadfast, Unmovable,
Always abounding in the will of God.
What's your name?
Your name is Strelsa, God's sparkling star.
Make him call you by your name.
Don't let him call you honey.
He's just trying to warm you up to get your money.
Don't let him call you baby. Baby, maybe.
It's his term for every woman; he greets on the streets.
Make him call you by your name. What's your name?
It's not whore or witch.
So stop scratching, when you don't itch.
Make him call you by your name.
You are entitled to your claim to fame.
Make him call you by your name and

Proclaim his desire to surrender his agenda for yours.
Make him call you by your name and
Declare his willingness to sacrifice
For you like Jesus did.
Make him call you by your name.
What's your name?
Your name is Integrity, Open and Public.
Don't let him isolate you from your family and friends.
It's a clear indication that
What you see, is not what you are going to get.
Make him call you by your name.
Keeping the relationship a secret is a notable set up.
So Resist the Seduction.
Get up Ebony Queen,
Stand up Zipporah,
Shake yourself off.
Close the Candy Store.
Move on Africa Woman
And make him call you by your name.[47]

There is nothing I like better than having someone call me by my name. However, today I want to talk about a name that has more power than our names. And that name is Jesus! Let's take a look at the beginning of chapter three in Acts so that we don't miss a key point that has direct bearing on our interpretation of this text. This might help us to fully appreciate the quintessential significance and providential impact of the "times of refreshing" for our lives. With the "times of refreshing in mind" we are going to preach from the theme, "Call Me by My Name."

The Bible says that one day Peter and John were going up to the temple at the time of prayer—at three in the afternoon. It was prayer time. Now a man crippled from birth was being carried to the temple gate called Beautiful, where he was put everyday to beg from those going into the temple courts. When he saw Peter and John about to enter, he asked them for money. Peter looked straight at him, as did John. He said to the man, "Look at us! We don't have any money, but what I do have I give you, in the name of Jesus Christ of Nazareth walk."

Versus 1–6 describe the miraculous healing of a man who was crippled from birth. Everyday he was placed at the temple gate called Beautiful to beg for alms. Whether he was placed there by friends I don't know or whether he was placed there by some opportunistic pimps I really can't say. But the text says he was placed there every day to beg at the temple gate called Beautiful. And he was placed outside the sanctuary. What is notable is the fact that he was never invited into the Sanctuary to worship. He was merely left at the foot of the temple gate called Beautiful to beg.

It is likely that the beggar man was left at the gate Beautiful, because many of the Jerusalem Jews came through that gate to enter the House of worship. *Josephus* suggests that this particular gate was so stunningly beautiful, because it was made of "Corinthian bronze and far exceeded in value the other nine gates plated with silver and gold leading into the temple."[48]

My beloved Sisters, the existential reality is that all of us have been crippled from birth. We have been sitting at the temple gate called Beautiful unable to stand up for ourselves and walk. We are unable to walk, because the image of ourselves has been distorted, disfigured, and disabled by the original sin of our rebellious, ontological progenitors, Adam and Eve.

Not only has the perception of ourselves been distorted by the disobedience of Adam and Eve, but some of us have been crippled by the sins of our ethnological ancestors, grandma and granddaddy. We have been sitting at the temple gate called Beautiful waiting for Daddy to come home. The Mighty Temptations tried to help us face reality when they sang this song, "Papa was a rolling stone; where ever he laid his hat was his home. And all he left us was alone." Daddy is not coming home, sisters.

Some of us have been sitting at the temple gate called Beautiful waiting for somebody to come and do for us what we have not been able to do for ourselves. We have been waiting for Peter and John to come along and put some money in our hands and tell us that everything is going to be alright. But the truth of the matter is that they don't have any money. They are struggling to survive. They tell us to our faces, "Silver or gold I do not have." And we sit at the temple gate called Beautiful and wait. Not only have we been handicapped by the original sin of Adam and Eve, and the sins of our grandmas and grand-daddies, we have also been crippled by our own personal iniquities. We have been sitting at the temple gate called Beautiful whoring after false gods. We have been lusting after our neighbor's house, our neighbor's car, our neighbor's clothes, our neighbor's job, and our neighbor's spouse. We have convinced ourselves that it is okay to get our sexual healing outside the covenant of marriage. We have been crippled since birth and been sitting at the temple gate called Beautiful waiting.

But Peter understands what we refuse to appreciate is that it is going to take more than silver or gold to empower this beggar man to walk. Peter says to the man, "silver or gold I do not have, but what I have I give you, in the name of Jesus Christ of Nazareth walk." Peter knew what he had. He had been with Jesus; he belonged to the inner circle. Yet he had disowned Jesus. Peter knew Jesus was "the Christ." Jesus had confirmed Peter's affirmation of him when He responded, "Flesh and blood have not revealed this to you but my Father who is in heaven ... you are Peter/*Petros* and upon this rock I will be my church."

The Scripture tells us in chapter 2 of Acts that Peter had been filled with the Holy Spirit at Pentecost; he had received the gift of tongues, and he had preached with so much power that 3,000 persons had given their lives to Christ. Peter understood that it was not because he was so mighty, but it was through the power of the Holy Spirit that transformation, deliverance, and healing was taking place. He recognized that it was by faith in the name of Jesus Christ of Nazareth that a crippled man could get up and walk.

We, too, are able to rise up from our impotent places and walk. If we reflect deeply on the text, we can hear Jesus saying, "Call Me by My Name." If you call my Name, you will walk. Not only will you walk, you will be able to run. "They that call upon the Lord shall renew their strength. They will soar on wings like eagles, they will run and not grow weary; they will walk and not faint."[49]

Peter understood what he had. The Bible says, versus 6b–9, that Peter invoked the name of Jesus took the man by the right hand, helped him up and immediately the man's feet and ankles became strong. He jumped to his feet and began to walk. Then the man went into the temple courts walking and praising God. And everybody recognized him as the beggar man who used to sit at the temple gate called Beautiful, and they were amazed. This was the beginning of the story.

Dr. Luke the author of our text continues the narrative. He says in versus 11 that the beggar held onto Peter and John. He could walk, but he was still holding on. In my sanctified, psychological imagination, I suspect that he may have been holding on to Peter and John, because he was co-dependent. He could walk, but he wanted reassurance that this thing was real. He could walk on his own, but he was still holding on. Some of us are like that; we can walk, but we are still holding on … Who are you holding on to? God wants to raise you up and do a new thing in your life. When God does a new thing in our lives, people will come running to signify. Such was the reaction of the Jerusalem Jews. The Jerusalem Jews came running to see for themselves the miracle man. And Peter breaks it down for them. He said to them, versus 12–16:

Men ... why do you look surprised? Why do you stare
at us as if by our own power ... we have made this man
walk? The God of Abraham, Isaac and Jacob, the God
of our fathers, has glorified his servant Jesus. You handed
him over to be killed, and you disowned him before Pilate
though he had decided to let him go. You disowned the
Holy and Righteous one and asked that a murderer be
released to you. You killed the author of life, but God
raised him from the dead. We are witnesses of this.

Peter confronts the Jerusalem Jews and says, you did it; "you
killed the author of life." But understand this one thing. "It is
by faith in the name of Jesus that this man whom you see and
know was made strong. It is Jesus' name and the faith that comes
through him that has given this complete healing to him ..."

In versus 17–19 Peter continues, "Now brothers I know you
acted in ignorance," but this is how God fulfilled his promises
which had been foretold by the prophets, saying that his Christ
would suffer. When God makes a promise he keeps it no matter
what the opposition. The promise had been made in Genesis to
Abraham. We are living in the fulfillment of that promise. Peter
speaks to the Jerusalem Jews and urges them to call on the name
of Jesus. If they want to live in the fulfillment of God's promise, he
tells them to "repent" turn from their wicked ways, their lives of
sin, and rejection of Jesus. "Turn to God, so that times of refreshing may come from the Lord, and that he may send the Christ,
who had been appointed for you even Jesus."

Peter does not hold it against the Jerusalem Jews for their dis-
owning of Jesus. Jesus had said from the cross, "Father, forgive
them for they know not what they do." But now they know and
have another opportunity to make it right. Confess, and turn away
from sin. God will forgive you of your sins. Turn to God. Call on
the name of Jesus. There is power in the name of Jesus. "For at

the name of Jesus, every knee shall bow and every tongue shall confess that He is Lord." Turn to God so that times of refreshing will come.

An exegetical study of the phrase times of refreshing suggests several possible translations from the Greek. The times of refreshing may be translated as showers of blessing to refresh you; relief from distressful, burdensome circumstances, a state of cheer and encouragement after a period of having been troubled or (watch this) breathing spaces.

The only other place in the Bible where this expression is used is in Exodus 8:15. The NIV translation reads, "But when Pharaoh saw that there was relief, he hardened his heart and would not listen to Moses and Aaron, just as the Lord said." Eugene Peterson puts it this way in his contemporary rendering: "But when Pharaoh saw that he had some 'breathing room,' he got stubborn again." The issue for Moses and the Israelites was the plague of frogs. The frogs were every where; Dead frogs were in the peoples houses, in the court yards and in the fields. They were piled into heaps, and the land reeked of them. Stench was in the air. Pharaoh begged Moses to call upon his God to take the frogs away. And God answered Moses' prayer and Pharaoh had some breathing spaces.

The Jerusalem Jews in Acts chapter 3 had the stench of dead frogs reeking in the nostrils of their lives. In their arrogance and foolishness they had rejected Jesus. Peter admonished them to repent and turn to God so that the times of refreshing, breathing spaces, might come from the Lord. Peter understood that trials and tribulations will come in life and only the believers who call upon the name of the Lord will be saved. In the midst of trouble when it seems like the frogs have over taken your minds, your houses, and your kitchens, and the stench is everywhere. God will give you breathing spaces, some times of refreshing.

And the good news is "the Messiah indeed has come as the

glorified Servant, the Holy and Righteous One of God. But the Jerusalem Jews did not receive him as Messiah; they disowned him." The Messiah, Jesus, will come again versus 20–21 to restore his kingdom to Israel. (Romans 11:25–26). He will give us times of refreshing in this present age and in the Kingdom age to come. Jesus is coming back again to restore everything. Whether that will be a time of refreshing, for the Jews will depend upon their repentance and reception of Jesus as Messiah.[50]

When Jesus comes back, he will be looking for those of us who call him by his name. He will restore us to our true image. We will no longer be crippled sitting at the temple gate called Beautiful. Our image of ourselves will no longer be distorted, disfigured, or disabled. We will be beautiful and whole, because we will reflect the true image of God. We will walk in peace, joy, and love in that heavenly city, a New Jerusalem and a new earth.[51] This is the fulfillment of the promise God made with your fathers. Verse 25 He said to Abraham through your offspring all peoples on earth will be blessed (Genesis 12:3).

Notes

1. Carter G. Woodson, From the Preface of *The Mis-Education of the Negro* (New Jersey: Africa World Press, Inc. edition, 1990) xiii.
2. Exodus 1
3. Exodus 5
4. Exodus 7–11
5. Exodus 13–14
6. Numbers 13:1
7. Numbers 13:30b
8. Numbers 13: 31
9. Numbers 13:33
10. Numbers 14:12
11. Ben Witherington, *Women and the Genesis of Christianity* (Cambridge University Press, 1990) 99.
12. Robert W. Funk, Roy W. Hoover, and the Jesus Seminar, *the Five Gospels: The Search for the Authentic Words of Jesus* (New York: Polebridge Press, 1993) 325.

13. John 6:35

14. John 2:9

15. *Don't Bother Me, I Can't Cope* was the title of an off-Broadway play featured at the Morris Mechanic Theater, Baltimore, Maryland in the 1970's.

16. Lindsey P. Pherigo, *"The Gospel According to Mark,"* *The Interpreter's One Volume Commentary on the Bible* (Abingdon Press, 1971) 644.

17. Ibid.

18. Fr. *Stanisalo Loffreda* ofm—SBF Jerusalem, Welcome, *Capernaum: The Town of Jesus, A.D. 2000, Franciscan Cyberspot,* (1998) 1–2 of 6) internet [http://www.christusrex.org/wwwl/ofm/sites/TScpintr.html]

19. Ibid, The Village—description, 3 of 5.

20. William E. Hull preached a sermon entitled "Rescue the Perishing" at Mountain Brook Baptist Church, March 1, 1998. He gave me a copy of the tape when I was a doctor of ministry student in his class on Strategic Leadership.

21. Luke 2:41–49

22. Luke 4:1–13

23. Luke 4:24

24. Luke 4:38–41.

25. Luke 22–24.

26. Genesis 1:26

27. 1Kings 8:12, Judges 14:6ff, 1Samuel 11:6.

28. Walter A. Elwell, editor, *Evangelical Dictionary of Theology* (Baker Books, Michigan, 1984) 523.

29. Acts1:4–8.

30. *The Original African Heritage Study Bible: KJV*

31. Jeremias Joachim, *The Prayers of Jesus* (Fortress Press, Philadelphia, 1967) 73.

32. Brian J. Dodd, *Praying Jesus Way: A Guide for Beginners and Veterans* (University Press, Downers Grove, Illinois, 1987) 77.

33. Judson W. VanDeVenter, 1855–1939, "All to Jesus I Surrender," *AME Bicentennial Hymnal* (Nashville, 1984) 251.

34. Jan Milic Lochman, *The Lord's Prayer:* Translated by Geoffrey W. Bromiley (Grand Rapids, William B. Eerdmans Publishing Company, 1990) 125.

35. Psalm 51:10

36. Luke 4:1–2

37. Herman C. Waetjen, *Praying the Lord's Prayer: An Ageless Prayer For Today* (Harrisburg, Trinity Press International, 1999) 93

38. Joachim Jeremias, *The Lord's Prayer:* Translated by John Reumann (Philadelphia, Fortress Press, 1964) 29.

39. James 1:13

40. Joachim Jeremias, 29

41. Rev. 20:4b

42. Philippians 4:12–14

43. Luke 11:9

44. Luke 11:13

45. Revelation 21:1–4

46. *AMEC Bicentennial Hymnal* (Nashville, The African Methodist Episcopal Church, 1984) 413

47. Patricia A. Outlaw, an original poem written March 27, 2004

48. John B. Polhill, "Acts," *The New American Commentary* (Broadman Press, Nashville, 2001) 126–127.

49. Isaiah 40:31

50. John B. Polhill, 135.

51. Revelation 21:1

About the Author

Dr. Patricia A. Outlaw, a native of Baltimore City, Maryland, is an Itinerant Elder in the African Methodist Episcopal Church and a Licensed Psychologist. She presently serves as an Associate Professor of Divinity at Beeson Divinity School, Samford University, Birmingham, Alabama.